LEARN

Portuguese

WORDS

sky
o céu
(doo SEH-oo)

friend
o amigo
(oo ah-MEE-goo)

game
o jogo
(oo JO-goo)

bird
o pássaro
(oo PAH-sah-roo)

soccer ball
a bola de futebol
(ah BOH-lah dee foo-TEE-bo-oo)

BY M. J. YORK • ILLUSTRATED BY KATHLEEN PETELINSEK

Published by The Child's World®
1980 Lookout Drive • Mankato, MN 56003-1705
800-599-READ • www.childsworld.com

Acknowledgments
Translator: Carolina Alvim Ferreira, MS,
University of Wisconsin–Madison

ISBN 9781503835832
LCCN 2019944694

Printed in the United States of America

ABOUT THE AUTHOR

M. J. York is a children's author and
editor living in Minnesota. She loves
learning about different people
and places.

ABOUT THE ILLUSTRATOR

Kathleen Petelinsek loves to draw
and paint. She also loves to travel
to exotic countries where people
speak foreign languages. She lives
in Minnesota with her husband, two
dogs, and a fluffy cat.

CONTENTS

Introduction to Portuguese

Portuguese is the language of Portugal and Brazil. Many Portuguese speakers live in eastern and southern Africa. Portuguese speakers live in the United States, too. More than 200 million people speak the language worldwide.

Portuguese is a Romance language. It developed from Latin, the language of the ancient Romans. Spanish, French, and Italian are other Romance languages.

European Portuguese and Brazilian Portuguese are different in several ways. Some terms are different. The order of some words in sentences is different, too. But the biggest difference is how vowels sound.

Portuguese uses the same alphabet as English. Most letters are pronounced the same, but there are some differences. This book shows how Portuguese words are pronounced in Brazil with a neutral accent.

Vowels

Vowels in Portuguese may be pronounced with a nasal sound, an open sound, or a closed sound, or they may be almost silent.

- A nasal sound comes through the nose.

- An open **a** sound is like f**a**ther or b**a**t. An open **e** sound is like b**a**y or b**e**t. An open **o** sound is like p**o**t.

- A closed **a** sound is like f**a**n. A closed **e** sound is like **e**ar or p**e**ople. A closed **o** sound is like f**oa**l or b**oo**k.

Accent Marks

- ~ a tilde means to make the vowel with a nasal sound

- ' an accent shows which syllable is stressed or makes the vowel sound open

- ʌ a circumflex shows which syllable is stressed or makes the vowel sound closed

Consonants

- **ç** sounds like **s** as in sat

- **ch** sounds like **sh** as in **sh**ine

- **h** is silent at the beginning of a word

- **j** sounds like **s** as in trea**s**ure

- **lh** sounds like **lli** in mi**lli**on

- **m** at the end of the word is nasal, like **ng** as in si**ng**

- **r** sounds like **r** in **r**oad, but trilled or rolled

- **nh** sounds like **ny** in ca**ny**on

My Home
Minha Casa
(MEEN-nya KAH-zah)

window
a janela
(ah ja-NEH-lah)

lamp
a luminária
(ah loo-mee-NAH-ree-ah)

bathroom
o banheiro
(oo ban-NYEI-roo)

bedroom
o quarto
(oo KWAR-too)

television
a televisão
(ah te-le-vee-zan-oon)

kitchen
a cozinha
(ah koo-ZI-nya)

cat
o gato
(oo GAH-too)

living room
a sala de estar
(ah SAH-lah dee es-TAH)

sofa
o sofá
(oo so-FAH)

chair
a cadeira
(ah kah-DEI-rah)

table
a mesa
(ah MEY-zah)

In the Morning
De Manhã
(dee man-NYAN)

dresser
a cômoda
(ah KO-mo-dah)

clock
o relógio
(oo re-LOH-gee-oo)

teddy bear
o bichinho de pelúcia
(oo BEE-shoo dee pe-LU-cee-ah)

doll
a boneca
(ah boo-NEH-kah)

pillow
o travesseiro
(doo trah-vee-SEI-roo)

bed
a cama
(ah KAN-mah)

blanket
o lençol
(oo len-SOH-oo)

At the Park
No parque
(Noo PAR-kee)

Let's play!
Vamos brincar!
(VA-moos brin-KAR!)

sky
o céu
(doo SEH-oo)

friend (male)
o amigo
(oo ah-MEE-goo)

friend (female)
a amiga
(ah ah-MEE-gah)

**MORE USEFUL
WORDS**

game
o jogo
(oo JO-goo)

sports
os esportes
(oos ees-POR-tees)

soccer ball
a bola de futebol
(ah BOH-lah dee foo-TEE-bo-oo)

bird
o pássaro
(oo PAH-sah-roo)

12

sun
o sol
(oo SOH-oo)

swing
o balanço
(oo bah-L'AN-soo)

cloud
a nuvem
(ah NOO-vein)

playground
o parquinho
(oo par-KEE-nyoo)

slide
escorregador
(oo ees-ko-he-gah-DOR)

water
a água
(ah AH-goo-ah)

pond
a lagoa
(ah la-GO-oo-ah)

flower
a flor
(ah FLOR)

duck
o pato
(oo PAH-too)

13

Around Town
Pela Cidade
(PE-lah see-DAH-dee)

library
a biblioteca
(ah bee-blee-o-TEH-kah)

firefighter (female)
a bombeira
(ah bon-BAY-rah)

Excuse me.
Com licença.
(kon lee-SEIN-sah.)

woman
a mulher
(ah moo-LEE-er)

man
o homem
(oo ON-mein)

police officer (male)
o policial
(oo po-lee-see-AH-oo)

street
a rua
(ah ROO-ah)

airplane
o avião
(oo ah-vee-AN-oon)

office
o escritório
(oo es-cree-TOH-ree-oo)

building
o prédio
(oo PREH-dee-oo)

bus
o ônibus
(oo ON-nee-boos)

MORE USEFUL WORDS

truck
o caminhão
(oo kah-mee-NYAN-oon)

train
o trem
(oo TREH-een)

stop
pare
(PAH-ree)

go
siga
(SEE-gah)

police officer (female)
a policial
(ah po-lee-see-AH-oo)

firefighter (male)
o bombeiro
(oo bon-BAY-roo)

15

How much does an apple cost?
Quanto custa uma maçã?
(KWAN-too KOOS-tah UN-mah mah-SAN?)

MORE USEFUL WORDS

please
por favor
(poor fah-VOR)

Thank you!
Obrigada!
(o-bree-GAH-dah!)

You are welcome!
De nada!
(dee NAH-dah!)

How are you?
Como você está?
(KOH-moo vo-SE ees-TAH?)

I am well.
Estou bem.
(es-TOO-oo ben-in.)

head
a cabeça
(ah kah-BEY-sah)

body
o corpo
(oo KOR-poo)

hand
a mão
(ah MAN-oon)

floor
o chão
(oo SHAN-oon)

leg
a perna
(ah PER-nah)

foot
o pé
(oo PEH)

My Birthday Party
Minha Festa
De Aniversário

(MEEN-nya FES-tah dee ah-nee-ver-SAH-ree-oo)

grandmother
a avó
(ah ah-VOH)

I am six years old.
Eu tenho seis anos.
(eoo TEN-nyo SE-ees AN-noos.)

grandfather
o avô
(oo ah-VO)

brother
o irmão
(oo eer-MAN-oon)

sister
a irmã
(ah eer-MAN)

cake
o bolo
(oo BO-loo)

MORE USEFUL WORDS

one **um** *(UN)*	eleven **onze** *(ON-zee)*
two **dois** *(DO-ees)*	twelve **doze** *(DO-zee)*
three **três** *(TRE-ees)*	thirteen **treze** *(TRE-zee)*
four **quatro** *(KWA-troo)*	fourteen **catorze** *(kah-TOR-zee)*
five **cinco** *(SEEN-koo)*	fifteen **quinze** *(KIN-zee)*
six **seis** *(SE-ees)*	sixteen **dezesseis** *(de-ze-SE-ees)*
seven **sete** *(SEH-tee)*	seventeen **dezessete** *(dee-ze-SEH-tee)*
eight **oito** *(OEE-too)*	eighteen **dezoito** *(dee-ZOI-too)*
nine **nove** *(NOH-vee)*	nineteen **dezenove** *(dee-ze-NOH-vee)*
ten **dez** *(DEH-ees)*	twenty **vinte** *(VEEN-tee)*

family
a família
(ah fa-MEE-lee-ah)

uncle
o tio
(oo TEE-oo)

aunt
a tia
(ah TEE-ah)

Happy Birthday!
Feliz aniversário!
*(fe-LEES
ah-nee-ver-SAH-ree-oo!)*

I love you!
Eu te amo!
(eoo TEE AN-moo!)

mother
a mãe
(ah MAN-een)

father
o pai
(oo PAH-ee)

presents
os presentes
(oos pre-ZEIN-tees)

cousin (male)
o primo
(oo PREE-moo)

cousin (female)
a prima
(ah PREE-mah)

De Noite
(dee NOI-tee)

MORE USEFUL WORDS

Today is Friday.
Hoje é sexta-feira.
(o-JEE eh SE-ees-tah FEY-rah.)

Yesterday was Thursday.
Ontem foi quinta-feira.
(ON-tein fo-ee KIN-tah FEY-rah.)

Tomorrow is Saturday.
Amanhã é sábado.
(a-man-NYAN eh SAH-bah-doo.)

Good night!
Boa noite!
(bo-ah NOI-tee!)

bathtub
a banheira
(ah ban-NYEI-rah)

I am tired! (male)
Estou cansado!
(es-TOO-oo kan-SAH-doo!)

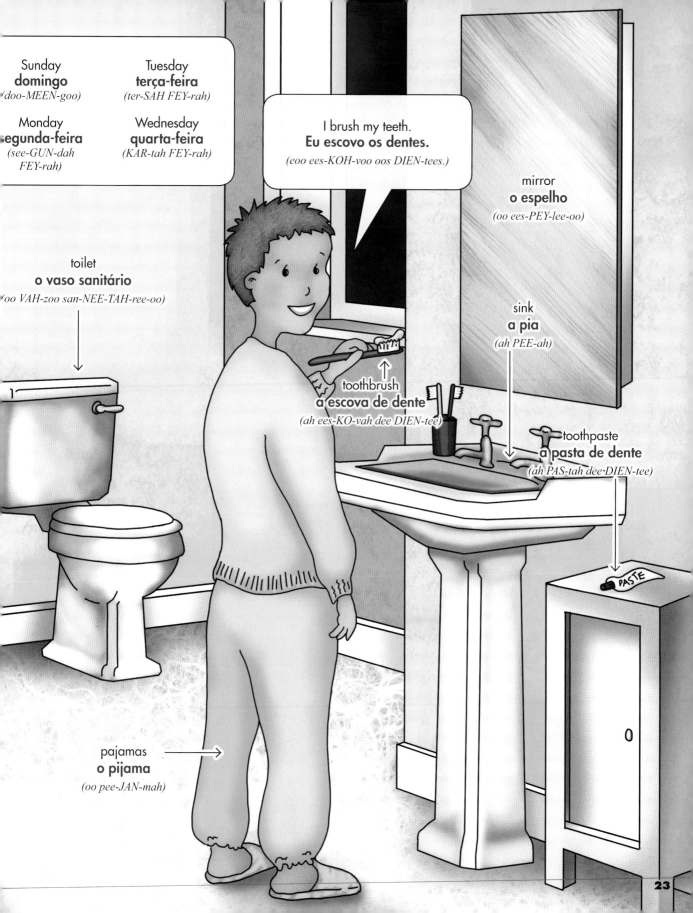

MORE USEFUL WORDS

Yes
sim
(seen)

No
não
(nan-oon)

ten
dez
(DEH-ees)

twenty
vinte
(VEEN-tee)

thirty
trinta
(TREEN-tah)

forty
quarenta
(kwa-REN-tah)

fifty
cinquenta
(seen-KWEN-tah)

sixty
sessenta
(se-SEN-tah)

seventy
setenta
(se-TEN-tah)

eighty
oitenta
(oi-TEN-tah)

ninety
noventa
(no-VEN-ta)

one hundred
cem
(SEYN)

January
janeiro
(jahn-NEI-roo)

February
fevereiro
(fe-ve-REI-roo)

March
março
(MAR-soo)

April
abril
(ah-BREE-oo)

May
maio
(MAH-ee-oo)

June
junho
(JOON-nye-oo)

July
julho
(JOO-lee-oo)

August
agosto
(ah-GOS-too)

September
setembro
(se-TEM-broo)

October
outubro
(ou-TOO-broo)

November
novembro
(no-VEM-broo)

December
dezembro
(de-ZEM-broo)

winter
o inverno
(oo een-VER-noo)

spring
a primavera
(ah pree-mah-VEH-rah)

summer
o verão
(oo ve-RAN-oon)

fall
o outono
(oo ou-TO-noo)

good-bye!
tchau!
(tee-AH-oo!)